DOG SLEEPS

DOG SLEEPS

IRRITATED TEXTS

———

MONTY REID

NeWest

Canadian Cataloguing in Publication Data
Reid, Monty, 1952 –
    Dog sleeps

ISBN 0-920897-35-5
1. Title.
PS8585.E53D6 1993   C813'.54   C93-091715-4
PR9199.3.R45D6 1993

Credits
Editor for the Press: Douglas Barbour
Cover and interior design: Diane Jensen
Cover photo: Robin Broderick

NeWest Press gratefully acknowledges the financial assistance of The Canada Council; The Alberta Foundation for the Arts, a beneficiary of the Lottery Fund of the Government of Alberta; and The NeWest Institute for Western Canadian Studies.

Printed and bound in Canada

NeWest Publishers Limited
Suite 310, 10359 - 82 Avenue
Edmonton, Alberta T6E 1Z9

for Pat and her sisters

CONTENTS

AGAINST TRAVEL

The day of pilgrims is over.

Janet Flanner

uninhibited restlessness

being, away from home, a restlessness of the subject, uninhabited,
as if something should happen, something increasingly dense, more
thorough than has been envisaged, the grunt of traffic in the street
below the hotel promises

a way to mutter I, as the subject I suppose is a promise, a means of travel, an enabling of something to come about, to become subjected to the present, the current evening, which is Saturday, and I have come to this city on an unplanned trip I would describe nevertheless as business if I had to explain it, at least someone else is paying for it

and made the reservation in this paralytic hotel, so quiet inside, soft jazz on the radio, thick carpets, a ruin of satin pillows on the bed that makes it look edwardian parlour and something I have never not had in a hotel room before, no tv and no phone, none of that insistent mysticism that says you can be found, you can be in touch, this persistence of you

as if the city were full of your remains, and you keep stumbling across them and the footsteps, perambulatory ghosts, so untouchable in the hall

although the traffic noise from outside infiltrates the rooms, all those people moving

although the sound of traffic is inhuman, imported noise filling up the space where people were, the noise of their origins, perhaps there is some spectrometry that could track this, the way old light is partitioned with the elements of its source, its mineral separations like the expansion joints in a sidewalk

upon which I spent the afternoon walking and so hardly have or
make the opportunity to talk to anyone, except in the course of
what I have loosely come to call business, until someone on the
street, it was almost noon and he said when are you going to do
something about this weather?

it was hot already and I just looked at him, surprised, and he giggled
and kept walking and what *was* I going to do about it? I just kept
walking up the hill, sweating

and although I am pleased to walk this was a business trip, that
distinction, if you pay for it yourself it can't be fun
it just has to be tax deductible

unless you believe in that vagrant conjunction known as business
and pleasure, which travel agents insist is possible, even necessary,
and combine them on your ticket, wanting to assure you that you
can come back, and collect points both ways

but I was thinking of pleasure as escape, of a place always no longer
livable, of travel that always progresses towards the conceptual,
and was

nonetheless walking up the hill to a bookstore which was, I admit,
somewhat outside the normal parameters of my business in this
city, which was why I didn't take a cab, and I paid for the books
myself, and saved the receipts

and wondered whether I could get them all across the border but of
course this wasn't a problem, the border might as well not have been
there

I was aware all the time that I was here on behalf of someone else
and to make it worse, even replacing someone who had gotten
tonsillitis at the last moment and couldn't make the trip and we
were only able to transfer the ticket into my name by threatening to
take our account elsewhere, assuring the agent that pleasure had
nothing to do with it

so even in the course of business when I showed up for appointments
no one was expecting me, although they recognized who I was
supposed to represent and so business could be conducted, the way
traffic is conducted on the street by some motor of extravagant
energy that creates only the image of motion

where I am, no one knows me

where I have departed from is where I would be recognized

is this not the sound of traffic in the street below? a street missing
its traffic, the long hiss of departure after departure

is this not the reflective surfaces of airports, the lucite and mirrors
and brushed metals, alloys, the skin of the fuselage, and heat
reproducing itself as waves on the runway, disappearing in front of
you, as if you were
merely the image of this displacement

I want to be present the same time as

this gloss of sweat on my skin disappears

and already I am looking, through the furniture of this room,
through drawers that slide open so carelessly, guides broken off
inside although the cabinet itself is solidly made, through lists of
local discounts, campgrounds, museums

as if there is something missing from this room, a vacancy, which I
could occupy, which would perhaps help to define what I have
departed from, to reconfirm where it began

as if home is always something taken from the dresser, why think it
as something left, or as some rehabitable space, made possible only
by what will occupy it, the you I am always missing, a stasis that
moves, what is it

I am writing as

I was thinking of paralytic, if it means to loosen then I am a loose
woman, lost on the world

on this trip, which is to last only a few days, I have not even bothered to reset my watch, I just know that here I am always an hour behind, it never bothers me except when I first wake up, the traffic noise does it, there, outside my window

there is nothing special about here, it is just one of the many places that would be different if you were part of it, in this all places are the same

even though the spontaneous demonstration in the streets when the troops were airlifted into Central America was a nonevent there were how many hundred arrests

a stoppage

to let the word open

I sit in the room and read the books I got at the bookstore, they all
seem to be about where I have gone, what I keep disappearing into,
other words,

at midnight I am restless and want to go out for something to eat,
the hotel also has no restaurant, although it serves fruit and
croissants and coffee in the morning, so I get up and walk around
outside and the restaurants are either closed or full and I am afraid
to walk very far, the protesters continue to gather, around fires in
the squares, and there is an ecstatic prickle on the skin of this city,
so I come back to the room hungry but tired and notice for the first
time the way the paint has been scratched off the door posts,
probably when they moved the furniture in

I don't care, staying in this room, there is no one else here with me,
you might be worried about that, last night beautiful men in
leathers stood on the bridge and I hesitated but there is just
the traffic

and I am motionless

and an hour late

to lose oneself is not the same as
not to find one's way

it is not yet midnight, by my watch, and I am thinking about
fucking you, perhaps to compensate for thinking about those men
last night, and that is how I thought of it, aggressive, hoping it could
be something stepped outside of, a room, if it is spacious enough
you do not need to turn, not even back, not even to find one's way

in a departure lounge, the faint buzz of metal detectors

I no longer like to fly

so here I am, not completely myself, horny, waiting for something
to happen, I suppose it disperses me, across the trajectory of those
route maps in the in-flight magazines tucked into the seat with the
barfbag

disappearing over the horizon with its plenitude of description, over
an area long-ago characterized as "here be dragons" and more
recently as "unorganized"

as they have also taken to characterizing the weather now, when it
doesn't perform according to spec and the flight is delayed, as I have
also come to consider myself

my feet sore and persistent

as if that is where some concentration of the subject might occur, even here, in the knowledge that I could stay, travel a cancellation of itself, an immobility, that makes here the place impossible to leave

so it is not even return that makes arousal possible, but this excess stasis, and still I am excited, by this not knowing, in this city by the fog

last night, out walking, I saw a hotel burning

there is nothing to see

I have given up sending postcards

wish you were here

there is no more place, nothing so easy to administer

only the indiscriminate texture of transfer, immediate copies,
duplicates of the self loosened onto every destination, thinking they
are all home

just as what is represented is lost

just business, here's my card

so what is real is just the visible
on back-order

why would you expect it to be any different?

or why I should think of it as a place, an appointment where they
are probably expecting someone else

with whom they can cut a deal

and yet in my need for you every city is the same

"The whole business of eroticism is to strike to the inmost core of
the living being, so that the heart stands still"

I wish I could buy a t-shirt that said that in this town

so who needs desire, if you have to travel to find it, apprehending
yourself elsewhere, that hopelessness, like all those aging men, my
children, making their way back to me, they travel then they die

the deal closes

as if it were some door

through which we go out to celebrate, no one offers to drive me so I come back to my room on the subway, I was tired and dozing and felt someone brush against my foot and looked up, a cadaverous woman, her teeth protruding, her breath stank, she had to get to the hospital, she showed me her photo id and half-hidden, a card that read HANDICAPPED, could I lend her some money, it cost twenty dollars just for the hospital to look at her

this woman desperate to be seen

and I could barely keep my eyes open, she leaned over me, put one hand on my shoulder, smiling because I was just waking up, then she put her other hand on the wrist of my right hand, which was resting in my lap, I looked at her face and felt repulsion and the twinge of arousal, I shook my head, she walked away

I watched her through the flawed layers of glass between cars, the
shifting light splayed into colours, the bars its cage of signature,
and I thought of that distance between us not as something variable,
as if there were two movable points, but as something static,
planar, a consistent quality, no longer a function of the space, but
the space, and yet this woman is there

how one would represent an idea of oneself, a card with
HANDICAPPED on it?

what is it they say distance
is supposed to do?

distance destroys plot

also

travel is the indivisible

track of desire, a map of gold card purchases, the interest on what
you owe, its trajectories binding the system against the terrain,
which is why I have been sent, to drag the web behind me

I saw the look on the handicapped woman's face as she moved
through the subway, its wake of particles no longer there, or even
alive, convinced she only needed to be visible

every dream of escape that hopeless, until it can no longer be dreamt
as escape, but is pushed out on the streets of this here and no other

my feet hurt

I was going back to my room with a signed contract, those
indecipherable signatures, the deal slammed shut

I'll soak them in a tub of hot water
and won't be moving again

WRITING-ON-STONE

Haunted places are the only ones people can live in.
                            Michel de Certeau

The landscape is not made into this, it is unmade, flutes of wind, a
substitution of water, reduce it, its signatures reduce it, and then
there is room for the ghosts to inhabit it

                                and altho you may entertain the
thought, out of courtesy or rational self-interest, that there are no
ghosts, there is a space for them, here in the valley's cavity, the
ribs rising on either side, the skin fallen away
                                into which we spill, thinking we
are too light, too permeable to even be real, but in the arid pod of
this valley we rattle against the walls where the inscriptions tease
us with names, what passes through them,
                        the hunts, celebrated births, tawny sandstone
palisade against which the cattle gather

ii

for shade just outside the park boundaries within which,
although it is a protected area there is no greater urge than to place
a name on this stone, soft enough that a broken poplar twig can
scratch it
                        and it may have meant something,
somewhere, to have the word inscribed upon the rock
but here it is just a way to undo its surface and let another image of
ourselves out
                        paler if more recent, but equally indifferent to
preservation, you can see it echo off the terrain wavering with the
heat and so many subtractions, until it disappears
among the apartmented rock, a

iii

futile gesture but one so intimate and prohibited there can be no
returning from it once it has been done, all you can hope is that
there is no visible connection between what you have exposed
and you
                          to expect anything
more would be foolish and even dangerous, the way the deer,
a mule doe, surprised in a pocket canyon just up from the river,
panicked,

          her black atonal hooves clattered against the rock debris
and then came straight at you, the only way to escape,
and you were standing in the mouth of the fissure as if you were
dreaming, you could have touched the rocks on either side,

          and the deer

iv

stopped abruptly just a few feet away from you, her eyes wild

and then you moved, I was yelling at you to get out of the way,
and when you did the deer just trotted by and disappeared into the
buffalo berry otherwise she would have run right through you

we were coming back from the Battle Scene, barely visible in the
discoloured rock, salts leaching out of it, a crystalline fuzz along
its vertical fractures, water percolating self-consciously through a
monument it has created to itself

     by removal

               these compacted sediments, austere with
their translation into granular light, their interior tensed against
the siliceous flakes even now carving ruin, decline from within,
every battle

V

a lost battle, and yet what is lost is freed to circulate among us, as
a space that insinuates itself, motile, within the enfigured stone

this is what any ghost would return to, not their histories however
written about, their deposition, their empty prehistoric vocabularies
of silence and identity

but their current charge, oxides graphed onto the cliff
face, irreversible, as if they accounted not only for the movement,
but the truth of this rock

just as the names at Signature Rock, that
way out of the canyon, where they hauled the wagons and ox-carts,
are the names of policemen a long way from home but standing
guard over the valley, vigilant

vi

for what has escaped, which slips into the shimmer of light bearing
the heat of their names

                         those desperate holes carved
in the weathering rock, collectively by some male need to have
something to prevent, the impossible
reality, native or recent arrival

          like bootleg whiskey and American cattle indifferent to
the parallel, that returns, once again towards this gap, Police
Coulee, towards the stone edges that accumulate, chimney and
eroded pedestal
                    the ragged fringe of something
not completely tactile through which the fat-bellied marmots,
expanding their range down the valley, waddle
nonetheless

vii

exposed to the hawks that are rarely seen but always suspected in
this landscape, red-tailed, mottled on the breast,
with the ironic talons that say an unprotected space
is a predatory space, top carnivore in a chain of repressed
but increasingly plentiful origins,

                              some of which

have never been recorded this far downriver, pushing down the
valley hidden from view as if it were the hollow parts of a body,
irreversible emptiness, the chamber
                                        that echoes in the heart
when a name is shouted, set in motion,
                        resonating with the breath
of the emptiness of those bodies it lies next to,
canals of brain and intestine, this space that eats you up,
the way willows by the river eat light out of the air

viii

and shiver in the breeze that eventually comes up in the late
afternoon, too long deferred
but gracious nonetheless
                              just certain that this
is where rapture is most deeply rooted, and it will have some, again,
the silver undersides of the willow leaves

                              a slight fussiness

on the river's surface, is the track of its attention, which is always
mobile but never moved, altho it too has maintained some
illusions, it tells
itself, once, a long time ago
                              but still within the living
synapses of decomposing stone, it was taken out of itself,
transported, drifting in a geological current and deposited
in this hierarchy of strata, its surface scratched away,
so the working order is visible

                              to which we keep returning

ix

hoping to find something lost, the field marks of home, none of
which can be identified in this inhibited terrain upon which nothing
is supposed to be written

                         but everything is

so it passes through and is gone,
rousing the bats, long-tailed, into prim vectors
across the technicalities of evening, its bugs and flowers,

and the government funded bat-study van leaves the campground
ahead of a ghost of dust, within which the campers have also begun
to stir, at least the paba-coated adults,

                              their sunburnt kids
have been tubing in the shallow water even in the heat,
out of their chronic afternoon fatigue, leave the shade,
come to walk barefoot, tentative on the trucked-in

X

sand along the riverbank, in their dry and loosely defined tracks is a
generic desire, not something of their own, yet, although the
imprints look vaguely familiar, in the way sand spills
back into them
                    softening them, making them indistinguishable
from the other proven formulae, the complex feeding trails
of the selves
                    which are always ahead of the words,
there with their hunger, among the sandstone turrets silhouetted by
the light draining from its pools in the valley

through which the bats skirt, and in the empty
castellated spaces where you might think some mystery
has been held, perhaps against its will
                                        if that is what it has had
all these years, there is only a seep of water, letting itself down
like a sheen

xi

of hair through the rock, impossible
to climb, although evening is the best time to explore the formations
even then you will not find the rungs that take you to her chamber,
there is

      none, no habitable space in the rock, only outside it,
among its disfigured shapes that imagine the darkened air as the
mother of their beautiful disfigurement, out of which track the
names carved one

         upon the other, each one deeper into the rock,
a reduction of the gods a few Blackfoot recognize still,
insistent upon their visibility, in
their unlikeness

         to anything

xii

and for them this is an unpassable ground

                              the old native couple
waited in a camper parked on a ridge overlooking the valley,
where we scattered with our insistence to see the names,

the need to touch the rock, with
our acidic fingers, our own disprovable gods, that interminable
list of what is ours, and they must have laughed as this place
disappeared under our hands
                              which is where all places go,
unstable, right through us

the shortest route to the outside, and in the mucous at the back
of our throats is an unforgettable impression of what they were, as
if we were getting a summer cold, and we swallow
the sour taste and look

xiii

at them again, here with their signage, the self-guiding trails that
are never the shortest routes to the in-situ displays
but get there just the same and yet
                     who could sneer
at this interpretable world,
traversed by so many ordinary practices, none of which pretend
to see everything

                  who listen attentively as the park naturalists,
underpaid summer employees, describe the rare fauna, scorpions
and the inch-long sculpin probing evangelically up the Mississippi
drainage, unknown in any other Alberta river
                              listen with belief, and a
requisite ignorance of what is believed, so that as they sit on their
blankets in the

xiv

flicker of the campfire program, ducking as bats fret at the edges
of the light, they begin to suspect they do not know
what they know

　　　　　　　　　and the only way for them to say exactly
what they mean is to be protected and described by some agency
with unlimited budget and so they go again, even in their dreams, to
scratch at the rocks, as if that would be evidence

but instead the lines are just where
the surface disappears, as if this one-time Spanish possession,
claimed because of the direction of its drainage, south into the Gulf
of Mexico via the Mississippi

　　　　　　　　　　　　too thick to drink
but too thin to plow, was all exposure

　　　　　　　　　　　and once again
we build outposts among removal

XV

                                    as the water fills the Gulf
with an insistence that it cannot satisfy any claims, and so was
given to the French who ceded it to the British who also relinquished
title

    and now ownership is divided equally among the names the
rocks
release the way ghosts condense out of the fog that schools among
the willows and then disappears into light

and the threads and twigs and detritus of memory
are made of such release,
                    hardened into a nest, a space it has already
abandoned, and the inhabitants have migrated and their footsteps,
even those filling with sand, are all that is left of their

xvi

bodies, the personal effects of a
legible world that can only be seen when what has made them is
gone, as the name appears, "... a peculiar whiteness being about the
color of a cup of tea with the admixture of a tablespoon of milk.

From the color of its waters we
called it the Milk River," Lewis and Clark 1805, or the Blood word

Kenushsisuht
"little river"

                                                and still the invisible erupts
like this unauthorized gap represented in the earth, potential desert,
its stack of implacable particles

                                    fine-grained lapse of the air,
that turns the everyday into a haunt of ghosts, whose ceremonial
remnants, still hung in a ragged

xvii

poplar gripping a crack in the valley wall, were just a red shirt and
some two-by-fours, left there, to tangle the wind, and no one
could describe its meaning or its necessity, only that it was a
cleansing

               although the elders let a park ranger watch
from the base of the wall as they climbed into the fissure
and came down again, intact, the ceremony
performed and two weeks later, the shirt faded, the old Blackfoot
couple still watch from the ridge as the proprietary
phantoms walk the landscape in our skins, as if we were the tombs
that ensure the sacredness of this ground

complete with cowshit and rabbit skulls

xviii

among the river's oxbows, its pastoral accumulations protected by
the city's need to represent such a space, with its wardens,
restricted sectors, administration, as a preserved innocence
even as it inserts, among

                     the goblins in the rock, its own blind
laws, and we are the shape of those ghosts, blind, touched with
space, all that carries the divinities with our memory and need,
our opaque bodies inscribed with names, unreadable

names, we are the gods for someone else
and what could cure us, treat us with recognition, who would be the
gods for us, if

                we wanted them,

xix

tracked them to the riverside and lost them there, let the sweet
milk disguise their passage, their hunger, although their voices wait
out the heat beneath the low-brush canopy across the water
that's what the field guides say

                let them go,
and then dance, ecstatic, in the moonlight
translated as a platform of quivering foxtail on the flats stretched
beyond the river, all mad surface, even when we hear them
the prayer of their

            consumption,
which is the sound of a body being touched, even within
the softly glowing nylon of our tents and the gas-generated caves of
motorhomes, against whose blinds the shadows flicker and upon

XX

which the moths beat audibly with their powdery frustration,
as the credulous darkness gathers and the saturated river,
unmoored, drifts away among the recitations of sandstone, the
analytic

       shores of an interior seaway

                its dreams
of intrusion and regress they themselves are the only acceptable
evidence of, and which we occupy
effortlessly, not as loss, but as a presence, celebratory

        anthropological
rags flapping with their washed-out monthly reds in the wind that
sucks into the vacuums of Writing-On-Stone it would like to believe
unnatural, the redemptive nooks

it has inscribed as what nature abhors, but what is

xxi

natural here is what has gone, ninety-nine per cent of all the species
that ever lived have disappeared
                                        escaped through us
into an uncreatable place that survives our every effort to
explain it except with the inexhaustible practice
of our lives, their sediments

borne in the chalky water of
this river that always changes its course, around obstacles deposited
by itself and out of that it has made its slow beauty

the empty names of all the names

BLIZZARD WALKS

The point is to get out of the antithesis between mother and father,
this revolving door between the regressive maternal warmth
and the icy paternal outside.

                                Jessica Benjamin

i

      some dislocation   carnal space

drifts   in air   muscular   pulse

fleshed zone

nothing   but projected weather

      all the traffic

blown in   those stalled cars   winter fetishes

     like shovels   booster

cables   I have learned   how to use

and in this how to ignore

        in the trunk

        the improbable lips   of a storm   kissed

late   in the year thus unfeared   as if it no longer
mattered
        so that it no longer   does   in the mouth

            a   slow drift
leaves hung   over edges   the matter flies apart

its tissue
        all previous   reports   inadequate

what I am is   this density

its fluctuating presence   not just

     its body   but what is made

of the body   over time   snowed-in plosives

meshed   agency   in which we walk   in ski
    pants   parkas

    mitts lined   with fingers

snuggled integument   as the lining   of any

weather is my   skin   which warms itself
    with itself   a learned
    continuity

    though in this

advisory   the threat of cold   unspoken

wet spring flakes   leisurely   simply   a means
of pleasure

        in such dense   intricacies

        of I am
you   I am you   all

        of the flakes   the crowd   of where

I am   my citizenship   and yet the same
        profusion

the storm a mass
        embodied

        abandon   without surface   space
where evasion   is among

the likely possibilities   its inferential walk   of

someone   who lives   among

    the warmed snow   deposited

against   such precise analysis   and yet

to forget

    is also   deadly

among heterogeneous   flakes thrashed up to

    drifts of catastrophic   detail

      what   oneself has become

    to wade in   surface not hard

enough to bear this weight   the body   is contiguous with

fall through

yet   fall in

ii

this storm is all surface all granular edge all geometric temperature
if I can't be the landscape can I be this weather

all hysterical sweep all apparat of breath all frigid projection if I can't
be climactic change I am the local conditions

all anorexic fragment all fracture all imaginary language if I am this
weather how fast will exposed skin freeze

all theoretical police all snow plows impossible to pass all ice fog
if I am the freeze can I be the tongue frozen to your brass prick

all limited visibility all specular facade all crystalline ritual if I
am the tongue I am the tongue of representation

all subzero recognitions all partial disclosure all ideal other if I am
the parts of a body am I the body

all disidentified highway all white pulse all wind chill expressed in
metric if I have been the body is there comfort in its idea

all stalled transit all frozen mains all the dogma of weather if there
is a comfort am I what slips through its inside unnoticed

all filaments of disappearance all arctic matrix if I am inside if I
am motherless am I the impenetrable construction

all moral gender immovable all omega bloc all sheared lug nuts of
control if I am impenetrable there is nothing to penetrate

all optic ratchet all the overbite of frost all mere drive if I am
nothing I am the nothing you require

all gravel all salt all old antifreeze all worn snow tires all chains if
what you require is your own death this is it

all want
if I can turn on you like this am I the natural

world

iii

He thought he saw lights and he thought he knew the country so he
got out of the truck and walked into the hard weave of the storm.
The bottom was falling out of the thermometer and visibility was
almost nothing. Yesterday it was melting. Would a woman do this,
or only a man? The next morning a search party headed by his
father found him, curled up in the snow. Around him a few
footprints were still visible, having gone, still going, in circles.

I remember going home from church in a bad storm when I was
young. We had an old car, a 1952 Pontiac, I remember because I
eventually learned how to drive in that car. We were on a country
road, raked by a metallic north wind, and almost blind. The car
stalled. A man, he wasn't my father, who had died several years
earlier, tried to start it again but couldn't. It was too cold to wait out
the storm, even though we had our heavy winter clothes. He got an
old gunnysack out of the trunk and wrapped it around his head,
turned up the collar on his overcoat, and set out down the road. He
thought there were farms nearby. The car cooled off rapidly and I
climbed over the seat to be beside my mother in the front. My feet
were getting cold. She took off my boots and held my feet under her
fur coat, where they stayed warm. But she too was beginning to
shiver. She slid behind the steering wheel, turned the key and
pressed the starter. The car started almost immediately. We crept
down the road, straining our eyes for the stalks of weeds that would
mark the ditch, hoping that we would see a farmhouse if we went
by one. We did see it, the bush around it deflecting the wind, and
we turned into the yard. He had just gotten there and was drinking
a cup of tea while the farmer started his tractor. What I remember
most is the dirt on his face. The gunnysack was an old potato sack
and the wind had whipped the dirt out of it. Against the blackness
of his cheeks his eyes were a glazed, mad white.

Soon after my grandmother died, grandpa came to live with us.
Mother was the oldest daughter. Where else could he go, she said.
He was a big man but his health was failing and he was beginning to
forget things. Even so, he accompanied us most places. One time a
bad storm blew up while we were visiting relatives in Quill Lake.
We left early, but by the time we had gone a few miles drifting snow
made the road difficult. We got stuck in a drift and a man got out to
shovel. He was not my father. Grandpa grew increasingly
uncomfortable as we waited. He was in the back seat with me. We
rocked the car free and got moving. But grandpa was badly agitated
by this time. Stop the car he said. No one wanted to stop because we
would get stuck again. But he insisted, demanding it, reverting to
his native and by now panicked German. We stopped. He got out.
My mother ran after him. He shouted in her ear and she came back.
A blast of frigid air crowded into the car behind her. He's going back
for grandma, he says we left her, she said. We turned the car around
and followed him, hoping he'd stay on the road. I remember him as
this ghostly, flickering figure, disappearing into the scud of ground
drifting. When he fell down we all ran to him and helped him into
the car. He fell asleep beside me, talking to grandma.

I was fucking him in the back seat, or he was fucking me, it wasn't
something we did together very often, out on the Army road in the
middle of a blizzard. Maybe I was seventeen by then, or maybe we
were just necking, would I forget? The road was just a trail and
nobody used it but something went flying by. By the time we got
our heads up to window level the cops were there. They'd been
chasing another car but decided to check us out instead. We hid the
booze but they could smell it and when they found out where I
lived, just a little ways away, they made us give them the keys and
walk home. Even now I can't conjure up an image of me walking in
the snow. It was as if when I was in it, I was no longer something I
could believe in. But I can remember the cold. I've never been so
cold. This was the man my parents wanted me to marry because
they thought I was going to get pregnant and I did. I was leaving
him when I found out my brother had been driving the car the
police were chasing.

A man I lived with but refused to marry said we could make it. I had
seen that look before. If you looked up you could see sunlight, at
least momentary lisps of it, but at eye level there was nothing but
snow, blown out horizontal. We drove in it for an hour, going
slower and slower, with our emergency flashers on. The radio kept
announcing road closures. But not this one. It was getting so cold
that our heater couldn't keep the windshield clear. We couldn't see
any approaches where we might turn around. He pulled, tentatively,
onto the shoulder. I wrapped a scarf around my head and stepped
out of the car. He thought there was an approach just behind us but
I would have to guide him to it. The wind pulled the scarf off my
face as soon as I stepped out of the car. I held on to it as if it was a
tow line. I was the opaque spot in the translucence of the storm. He
followed me, going backwards, for a few feet, then stopped. I waved
at him, then went back to the car. Pellets of snow stuck to my
eyebrows. My face was already freezing. Stay close he said, I
couldn't see you.

It was March and we expected a chinook and we got a blizzard. But it was one of those benign storms, that only serve to sweeten your expectation of spring. It snowed for thirty-six hours, dense wet flakes like the kiss of sediment settling out of a slow current. There was no wind but the snow was so heavy it swamped the town. Nothing moved for a while. Then people opened their doors and stepped out into it, thrashing their way to the streets. Cars sagged helplessly under the weight of it, like loaves of cooling bread. No one went to work, except the doctors, who got to the hospital on snowmobiles. But on the streets, all over, you could see the tracks of people floundering through the snow. The drifts were too high to fall into, so there were no angels, just the earthly trails. I walked with him through the ravine. It was like wading in a kind of dream whip. It soaked gradually through our clothes with the ghosts of the afternoon and I found I couldn't say anything to him.

DOG SLEEPS

*Though we keep company with cats and dogs, all thoughtful people are
impatient, with a restlessness made inevitable by language.*

Lyn Hejinian

the dog eats my underwear, never my husband's, it goes to the
laundry basket in the closet and mauls through it and pulls out my
panties and chews on the crotch

I've gone home from work to find a trail of ruptured panties
through the house, they lie there like shot birds, it leads me to this
speculation, gender is an acquired taste, all the panties have wet
ragged holes in the same spot, sucked on

not that it ever noticed the colours, and fabric didn't matter either,
there was no preference, although there were a few with a double
crotch that may have been more of a challenge but in the end, there
they were, scattered on the floor, practical as hunger

I've heard of edible panties before and maybe it wouldn't be so bad
to have them eaten off you

but to find them like this, empty of any pleasure, except for the
dog's, which perhaps could not tell the difference

this is especially exasperating if the panties are new, which is
frequent now, or particularly comfortable, like those soft cotton
ones that were supposed to be like men's, envy again I can hear
them say, or one satin pair I should've never thrown in the laundry,
I knew this would happen to them

it is always my discharge that attracts it, never my husband's,
although his shorts are more rank and crusty than mine are and are
just as available in the laundry basket

no, it goes through the basket the way it would go through a bowl
of dog chow, looking for the juiciest chunks and the rest of it gets
left for next time

or maybe it's because my underwear just looks better, all its textures
and exotic colours and patterns, its high cuts and its bits of lace, and
my husband just wears a uniform if soft grey upon which the
peckertracks are not always apparent

on me the stains are always visible

not that it needs to see them, I think it's going blind, but it can sense
them, smell them perhaps, or perhaps it is a sense of impossibility,
because the stains are the outside of fluids, their solid edges, upon
which is impressed the film of what body?

not just its desire but its extended presence, its containment, what it
scribes the edges of

and hardens in the sheet's threads so an image is fixed, an
environment I have been poured into, like the stains hard water and
not enough soap leave on the cups in the dishwasher

a residue, what they say luck is,
of design

I should be so lucky

my vagina is anything but sterile god knows its range of emission
and enclosure, so I'm not pretending to any purity and maybe that's
what identifies it, what attaches it, scented and labyrinthian,
detectable ribbons, so many entrances

at the threshold of none of which does this dog even hesitate, not a
contemplative shuffle

and I am surprised, still, at the precision of the attraction, it snuffles
at the bottom of the closet door when I do remember to close it, or
tracks the basket down to the laundry room, there's no refuge, even
moving it around all the time isn't any good, it moves too

this is the same dog that got out of the yard and came back half an hour later with a bloody sanitary napkin and sat in front of the gate chewing on it, barking every now and then to get let in, or at least to get attention

it has no shame, only appetite, and the neighbours saw the soggy fibres lying on the sidewalk and were disgusted and walked home to slam the lids down tight on their garbage cans

no way we were letting it in until it was finished

we've talked at times of "putting it to sleep," as if sleep has ever been something we could put to you, like a question, and who is the "we" here anyway, it's not my husband talking, ask the dog

it's always been housebroken but one winter it habitually tracked itself through the yard, dug its own frozen shit out of the snow and ate it, plug by meticulously formed plug

then it would come to the door and jump up and try to lick your face

I remember the reason I picked it out of the litter was it was the only one that didn't try to lick my face when I held it up. It just hung there in my hand whimpering while its mother prowled in the field

I hate to think what it would be like if I hadn't neutered it, even more aggressive and tactless probably

I remember it came home from the vet with a big white cone strapped around its neck so it couldn't reach down and rip out its stitches, looking for the fresh blood of its own displaced virility, the scent drove it silly

it couldn't even see its loss, blindered, it could see only in front of itself, and for a few days all it wanted to do was sleep and chew, maybe the urge to chew my underwear is just the reinscription of that need

and then it comes to the edge of my bed with those sad clouded
eyes and I let it in, why not, what's the point of holding out, and
once it's in there's no moving it, it may be undernarrated but it's
irreversibly real and so fat it can hardly jump up onto the mattress,
not that it ever comes when I call

I've pretty well given up any notion of power, it lies there
imperturbable and I can hear its stomach growl

indigestible

and its first impulse is to lick the bed, the dried-up petals, leakage,
salt map, where we have gone when I have gone
out of our selves

the fluid that drains out of me, drying on the sheet where it is a
mirror image of part of my body, thigh and buttock, a ghost of
something other than identity and he licks it, following the trail as if
it were a route to el dorado

and then the wet spot is wet again and it licks itself shamelessly a
few times and settles in to sleep

beside the oasis

how do you train a dog like this, god knows I tried, with chokechains and rawhide bones and walkies every night and sure it'll respond and when I think we're getting somewhere it gets into my underwear again

they told me a female would make a better pet, but I wanted this colour, this anarchic black, and all they had in black was male

when I look at the slick fur, its coils, its black suction, it could be a space around a thin edge of atmosphere, hard vacuum around what is breathable, the dream

try grooming that

on one hike out of the yard it got so full of burrs I just shaved its hair right off and then it wandered around like a plucked chicken, humiliated and pink but with the black already growing back, as if it could secrete its own emptiness

but it does dream, its nose twitches, and its feet, and sometimes a
whimper flickers along the back of its throat

I could think of it talking in its sleep

it has nothing to say

to me

I dream too, she and I were killing people and cutting them up and
boiling the bodies and carrying the swill out to the car in boxes and
it kept leaking out and I kept thinking her husband will notice the
stains on the upholstery, I guess he didn't but the dog came along
and started licking them

it snores, and farts in its sleep

so do all animals

except us

or so I am tempted to think, as when I thought everything that was
unmistakably mine was a kind of betrayal, and the deception was
not the body or its egress but in the edge of that thought, the way

in his sleep it is at the perimeter of something, his tracks circulating
at the edge of the yard, fenced in, you can see him trot, unreleased
but repetitive, checking the same possible routes outside

as if it were finding a space in which it could be himself, some
indescribable place it could mark that does not belong to me, and
there is no such space because I am in it, am it

and I am nothing if not describable

and criss-crossed nonetheless by the evidence of such need

it makes me sad

my parents wouldn't have a dog because of the hair, they said and I
have come to believe them, that they wouldn't, the hair it leaves
behind is the web of an unhygenic obsession, a network lingering in
the bottom of the tub, slowly congealing in the drain

or the way I find it, fibrillated in the cotton of my sheets, some ghost
of the real ruining the fabric, the fibres worn thin but oh so pure, as
if they had been pounded on the rocks by someone, by some
woman, in bare feet at the edge of a brown stream, as if that would
redeem it

and there have been times when I have taken the throw rugs and
tossed them outside because they are black with its hair and then I
noticed one spring how the chickadees kept coming to the rugs

and realized they were picking the doghair off it
and flying it back to their nests, so I went and looked and tucked in
the thickest sleeve of the lilac bushes, softly lined with a weave of
black hair was the nest with two precise eggs

and I remembered how it looked when I had shaved him, as if I had
peeled a nest away from some impenetrable secret

maybe someday I'll throw out the chesterfield

and cleaning up the hair I have come to think of myself as a past, or
the hollow space in which a past can sleep, a space that is moulding
itself as mine, under this fabric, which appears so clean and stiff but
is gradually being replaced, becoming infinite, without centre or
periphery, dog or his or

whose?

what I do know is pleasure is not your own

the dog never worries about it, its dreams are nylon, immense and
colourful, balloon or parachute, just oversize versions of my
underwear, the air enclosed, momentarily, as if it were a space with
an edge

a property line, and then saturated with my smell, my deposit, this
dog chews a hole in the nylon and falls

through

or tent, around the pole
which comes apart in sections and gets stored in another nylon bag
which has been waterproofed but it leaks, just like the tent

and now that I think of it, the dog chewed the corners of the bag out
too, that time we were staying out on the island and the ground
was alive with hornets, it was as if a breeze was constantly in the
short grass, and when it went to sleep the hornets burrowed into its
fur and began to bite

and we couldn't see them but the dog went crazy, running in a
panic around the yard in the darkness, biting at itself and finally
swallowing the hornets, which must have stung its stomach because
it began shaking and threw up a thin green vomit in the lamplight

for some
all of nature
may be equally edible

and when it died

and when it died it died with irony

because it could no longer eat, this thing that fed on everything
it starved

when I took it to the vet the first time the vet said it could stand to
lose a little weight and didn't do any tests

and two weeks later it couldn't eat at all and was so weak when it
lifted its paw to be scratched it fell over and when we insisted that
the vet check it again its veins had deteriorated so badly they
couldn't even hold a needle, when the plunger pushed down
through the syringe his leg simply ballooned, all the solution loose
in its undifferentiated body

and they had to pump antibiotics and dextrose into the hump of
muscle on its shoulder, it didn't even feel the needles

the postmortem showed kidney failure and a heart abnormality

so it is merely remembrance now, and even remembrance cannot
return to the amorphic, the dead are shaped only inside the living

when I picked up the body from the vet, it was in a cardboard box
and it seemed too small and I asked are you sure this is the right one
and they said no question but it was too light and I said please
check and sure enough, they'd given me the wrong body

the second time I didn't even ask.

I buried it in the silty willow-bound dirt beside the river and
discovered later a huge anthill nearby and imagined a city of
tunnels, through which the corpse is distributed through the earth

but even that, the elements returning, particle by ever smaller
particle, into the interstices of the earth, is wistful imagination

when I went back to the grave it had been dug up by some other
animal, a coyote or another dog, with its own hunger and across the
first snow of the year the fragments of such imagination were
scattered, tufts of hair, corrugations of ribs, joint knuckles,
cardboard

I gathered the pieces again and reburied them, deeper, in the frozen
ground

everything gets done twice

for the dog, for you
tragedy and farce

and perhaps the threads of what is left of the upholstery are a map
of this dismemberment, a reading of the tunnels, or even of the
hunger that distributed it over the snow

and in the fraying threads I can still smell the cloyed smell of wet
dog and altho I promised myself this I cannot yet search for new
furniture, cannot change, my smell also in these fibres

and I have washed the sheets and cleared the drain with lye and still
try to remember to keep my laundry locked up

not that it would stop the buildup, of attraction, of a story being
generated, gendered, but would enable it to begin telling, as if it
made a lost space into one that could be recovered

somewhere I have been but cannot recognize myself, altho the dog
looks at me in my sleep and I think it recognizes me but doesn't
care, I am just the particular woman whose presence it smells

and I am tempted to wake it nonetheless

THE LAST TIME I TALKED
TO A MAJOR AMERICAN POET

*The most fundamental changes in human evolution
must be viewed from both ends of the body.*

Stephen Jay Gould

The last time I talked to a major American poet she was boiling up
some shit to cover the testicles she collected from the stockbrokers,
I called them Scotch eggs, and she couldn't talk long on the phone
because she was worried the pot was going to boil over

and I said this is a story about blockage, not flow, and she said she'd
get back to me and she did.

She said go ahead but, you know, please hurry because I've got this
senator to worry about and I said well this is a true story, it's about
plumbing, the joining together of pipe, once lead pipe, which is
where the term plumb derives from, but now pvc and iron, you
know how materials change.

And what follows the joinery, sheer, into the earth, as the eye
running down rivers of type, or how it is caught, blocked, by the
irruption of the external, in the fitted together pleasure

excess in general.

♦

Yeah, so? the major American poet said. The toilet was a pastel,
frothy green, not very versatile when it comes to bathroom decor, or
resale value, but it looked fine when we moved in, especially after
we put in new cabinets and wallpaper to match. And it worked.
The toothbrush had a green handle, although this was only by
accident. We don't colour coordinate, although toilet and
toothbrush were often enough in close proximity, I mean you often
use them in the same room and in theory this should lead to a
certain overdeterminism.

But this was an old toothbrush. I used it for years, cleaning off the
daily plaque, pushing the wadded fibers of unidentifiable stuff from
the gaps. I hate that feeling, when you've got something stuck be-
tween your teeth and you keep worrying it with your tongue but it
won't come out. You know the processes of decay have already set in.

♦

Anyway, for years I depended on the green toothbrush and it
worked great but eventually the bristles softened up and it was
relegated to the role of bowl cleaner, for around the rim of the bowl,
or near the hinges of the lid, where men always splatter. If it was
just women using this toilet I'd probably never need to do this at all.
Just smile, act pretty, open the door, and clean the toilet said the

major American poet.

I was cleaning the toilet I said, but then the toothbrush fell in and instead of getting it out right away I thought I'd leave it 'til he got home.

Plumbing challenges his self-image.

◆

But of course I forgot about it and eventually had to pee and when I flushed the toilet, so how closely do you look before you flush, there was the green toothbrush coasting around in the current and I didn't think it would disappear but it did.

I knew we had a problem. There was no way it was going to get through the maze of a toilet bowl, it was just too rigid, and the bowl too full of meanders and backwashes and traps to let something like this go through.

◆

Waste always demands the most capacious of images. The increasingly abundant production of new wastes tests those that made it said the message left on Lynn Margulis's answering machine the last time I tried to talk with her.

The part of the world I live in has been called the empty quarter and its jurisdictions have actually lobbied to be the sites of waste disposal plants, to be made real by its phantasmagorical vapours.

It would be nice to think of this stuff as constantly moving, all that seductive flow, in the pipes your house is hung on, under the streets, through the vascular system of the city, even settling, particle by ghostly particle in the downriver ponds, where the condoms wash up on the shore. Don't you ever get mad at anything said the major American poet.

Waste demands the space in our cells I told her.

♦

But ordinary things don't flow, they plug up the circulation. I knew the green toothbrush was there because the toilet wouldn't flush properly anymore, at first it was just a case of a slightly slowed-down wash, just the slightest hesitation before that abstract rinse.

But it gradually got worse.

I went out and bought a snake from home hardware. I fed it into the toilet and jammed it and twisted it as hard as I could and for a while things seemed to clear up. But a few days later the same process repeated itself, the toothbrush never dislodged, the snake just worked the accumulated paper free.

♦

The inevitable happened. Who's paying for this call said the major American poet the last time I talked to her. Water came up higher and higher and finally spilled over the lip of the bowl. I threw down some old towels.

When it subsided it left deckle-edged clots of paper stuck to the outside of the bowl and it was apparent that we'd have to pull the toilet and see if we could get at the toothbrush from the other end.

He undid the urine-eaten bolts and lifted the bowl off its wax seal
and hauled it out into the front yard. The yard is heavily treed so no
one would be able to see, except for one neighbour, who of course
happened to be on her verandah at the time. She watched as he
hauled this heavy bowl out into the yard and assaulted it, with the
snake again, from both ends.

I said this would be a challenge.

◆

It must be like the brain in there, all those convolutions, all that
extra surface area, for whatever that's been good for, the toothbrush
hidden in the labyrinth, and needless to say, it wasn't moving.
So we took the garden hose and turned the water on full and the
spray to its most powerful and stuck that in at the base of the toilet.
Some one might think, said the major American poet, that this is art.
She said that to me.

For a while there was nothing except the sound of water sloshing
around and then of course it erupted out of the other end in a spray
of paper and hair and what was indisputably fecal material. We were
standing clear but it was still kind of revolting, spattered all over the
lilacs. Then we stood back and washed it off and tried it from the
top end. Same results.

We put on rubber gloves on and reached inside as far as we could,
nothing but greasy porcelain, the proportions of a body, curving out
of reach.

◆

Our neighbour was an elderly lady named Antonin Artaud and she had been watching, of course, and she finally came to the end of her verandah and called to us You need more pressure, as if this was news. Ideas are only the voids of the body she said. Try the car wash she said.

So we loaded the toilet bowl into the van and drove over. We closed all the doors to the stall, made sure we had a pocketful of change and pulled the toilet bowl out. It sat on the metal grate beside some clumps of mud that fell out of the wheel wells.

We turned the hi-pressure hose on it and for a few seconds the toilet just absorbed the water. Then it gushed out the other end, streaks of soapy liquid ran across the floor.

◆

The door opened and the carwash attendant came past, she probably couldn't see much in the steam anyway, and she didn't stop, she just kept going to one of the other stalls. But she came back again in a minute and this time she took a long look at what we had lying in the middle of her carwash.

I could get in shit for that she said.

◆

The toilet sat there on the grate, a pale obstinate green. Unhooked from the system. The last time I talked to Antonin Artaud she said just say shit to everything and go to sleep, that's what I do.

Short of breaking the bowl open we had no idea how to get the toothbrush out so we took it to the plumber who tipped it upside down and ran her heavy-duty toilet auger into it and said the only way to get that out is with a sledgehammer

So we looked at the fixture catalogues and discovered that the toilet was seaspray and no one made that colour any more so we ordered a white one, an american standard, and admired its smooth quiet action when it was installed.

Don't use my name in this said the major American poet the last time I talked to her. Someone might think I really said that.

♦

And we took the green bowl out to the dump and broke it open with a sledgehammer just as the plumber advised and sure enough there was the toothbrush, anything but clean. People might mistake me for the words I've written said the major American poet the last time I talked to her.

The gulls wheeled around like they were going down a drain.

And we bought this new waterpik guaranteed to shock your ass if you drop it in the toilet.

It makes me feel secure.